SandCastle™

First Rhymes

The Band in the Sand

Pam Scheunemann

Consulting Editor, Diane Craig, M.A./Reading Specialist

ABDO
Publishing Company

Published by ABDO Publishing Company, 4940 Viking Drive, Edina, Minnesota 55435.

Printed in the United States.

Credits
Edited by: Pam Price
Curriculum Coordinator: Nancy Tuminelly
Cover and Interior Design and Production: Mighty Media
Photo Credits: AbleStock, Photodisc

Library of Congress Cataloging-in-Publication Data

Scheunemann, Pam, 1955-
    The band in the sand / Pam Scheunemann.
        p. cm. -- (First rhymes)
    Includes index.
    ISBN 1-59679-451-8 (hardcover)
    ISBN 1-59679-452-6 (paperback)
        1. English language--Rhyme--Juvenile literature. I. Title. II. Series.

PE1517.S3598 2005
808.1--dc22
                                                                    2005048045

SandCastle™ books are created by a professional team of educators, reading specialists, and content developers around five essential components that include phonemic awareness, phonics, vocabulary, text comprehension, and fluency. All books are written, reviewed, and leveled for guided reading and early intervention reading, and designed for use in shared, guided, and independent reading and writing activities to support a balanced approach to literacy instruction.

Let Us Know

After reading the book, SandCastle would like you to tell us your stories about reading. What is your favorite page? Was there something hard that you needed help with? Share the ups and downs of learning to read. We want to hear from you! To get posted on the ABDO Publishing Company Web site, send us e-mail at:

sandcastle@abdopub.com

SandCastle Level: Beginning

band

hand

land

sand

stand

This is a .

This is a  .

This is .

See the .

She likes to  .

The band plays music.

This is a left hand.

The land is green.

The sand is brown.

Elly likes to stand.

The Band
in the Sand

There is a
magic land.

In the magic land,
there is a big hand.

The big hand
plays in a grand band
in the magic land.

The big hand
and his grand band
play in the sand
in the magic land.

When the big hand
and his grand band
play in the sand
in the magic land,
the cheering
people stand.

About SandCastle™

A professional team of educators, reading specialists, and content developers created the SandCastle™ series to support young readers as they develop reading skills and strategies and increase their general knowledge. The SandCastle™ series has four levels that correspond to early literacy development in young children. The levels are provided to help teachers and parents select the appropriate books for young readers.

Emerging Readers
(no flags)

Beginning Readers
(1 flag)

Transitional Readers
(2 flags)

Fluent Readers
(3 flags)

These levels are meant only as a guide. All levels are subject to change.

ABDO
Publishing Company

To see a complete list of SandCastle™ books and other nonfiction titles from ABDO Publishing Company, visit **www.abdopub.com** or contact us at:
4940 Viking Drive, Edina, Minnesota 55435 • 1-800-800-1312 • fax: 1-952-831-1632